AN IDEAL CHURCH: A MEDITATION

DENISE LARDNER CARMODY

1999 Madeleva Lecture
in Spirituality

PAULIST PRESS
New York/Mahwah, N.J.

Library of Congress Cataloging-in-Publication Data

Carmody, Denise Lardner, 1935–
    An ideal church : a meditation / by Denise Lardner Carmody.
        p.   cm.—(Madeleva lecture in spirituality ; 1999)
    Includes bibliographical references.
    ISBN 0-8091-3885-9 (alk. paper)
    1. Church—Meditations. I. Title. II. Series.
BV600.2.C336   1999
262—dc21   98-55906
                                                                    CIP

Published by Paulist Press
997 Macarthur Boulevard
Mahwah, New Jersey 07430

www.paulistpress.com

Printed and bound in the
United States of America

CONTENTS

Denise Lardner Carmody is the Jesuit Community Professor at Santa Clara University. Teaching and chairing *this* religious studies department are her two professional delights. Author of more than fifty books, she wrote many of them with the late John Carmody. They were the first couple to receive the John Courtney Murray Award for Excellence in Theology, given by the Catholic Theological Society of America in June, 1995. Her most recent book is *Organizing a Christian Mind: A Theology of Higher Education* (Trinity Press International, 1997).

A MEDITATION *An Ideal Church:* *A Meditation* An Ideal Church: A Meditation AN IDEAL CHURCH: A MEDITATION AN IDEAL CHURCH: A MEDITATION AN IDEAL CHURCH: A MEDITATION *An Ideal Church: A Medita* *tion* An Ideal Church: A Meditation AN IDEAL CHURCH: A MEDITATION AN IDEAL CHURCH: A MEDITATION AN IDEAL CHURCH: A MEDITATION *A* *n Ideal Church: A Meditation* An Ideal Church: A Meditation AN IDEAL CHUR CH: A MEDITATION AN IDEAL CHURCH: A MEDITATION *A* *n Ideal Church: A Meditation* An Ideal Ch urch: A Meditation AN IDEAL CHUR CH: A MEDITATION AN IDEAL CHURCH: A MEDITATION *An Ideal Church: A Meditation* An Ideal

In memory of
John Tully Carmody
(1939–1995)

With gratitude, for
Paul Lucey, S.J.

PREFACE

This book is a meditation on what our Christian church ought to be. It does not avert its gaze from what the church is, but regularly it muses about the better community that we could create. Behind this musing is the assumption that we live by ideals. We have a reach that exceeds our grasp, though sometimes we can grab the gold ring before heaven.

The gracious invitation to give the 1999 Madeleva Lecture stimulated me to think again about the community that I am serving, having returned to a Catholic university setting after twenty-five years. Much in our church is beautiful, but a considerable amount is dreck. To hone my judgment in particular cases, I have found it necessary to go back to the basics and rework some constitutional issues. What are the main features of the community that tried to pattern itself on Jesus' example and vision? What are the better developments that tradition has bequeathed us? Can we separate necessary things from accidentals? How ought we to understand such staples of

Christianity as scripture, sacrament, church governance, church teaching, social action, and spirituality today?

It helps me to have been a cradle Christian and to have spent considerable intellectual time outside Christian borders, studying the world religions. It helps me to have participated in the rise of Christian feminism, gaining some sophistication about what is admirable in it and what idolatrous. But, more importantly, it helps me to have met through the years many Christians from various denominations who loved the church critically. They have been the angels on my shoulder, encouraging whatever measure of balance I have achieved. My thanks to all of them—a great cloud of witnesses.

CHAPTER 1
GOING BACK TO GO FORWARD

From at least as early as the middle of the first
Christian century, when the apostle Paul wrote
his letters to the Corinthians, the church has
found itself in disarray. In that same period, Paul
quarreled with Peter about the extent to which
Gentile converts ought to be held to the precepts
of the Jewish law, while a generation later the
Johannine communities in Asia Minor split over
the issue of whether interior anointing by the
Holy Spirit was a sufficient control for Christian
ethics. Later centuries were similarly full of controversies and divisions: about the proper influence of gnosticism, about how to understand the
divinity of Jesus, about whether to readmit
people who had apostatized during persecutions.
By the medieval period, when the Eastern and
Western branches of the church split (1054), and
the papacy later moved to Avignon, disarray
could seem more prominent than unity. The

3

Protestant Reformation that split the Western church in the sixteenth century, the subsequent religious wars that bloodied Europe, and then the exporting of Christian divisions to Africa and Asia through colonialism made the modern period a time of constant wrangling.

As we Catholics begin our third millennium, we therefore ought to be nervous. On the one hand, this new era glistens with the possibility of new beginnings—a possibility that has seized the imagination of Pope John Paul II, who has urged on the church a commitment to evangelization. On the other hand, no less a group than the Society of Jesus, meeting in Rome early in 1995, has found itself confused and insecure about evangelization. As the Jesuit Father General, Peter-Hans Kolvenbach, put it then: "...everything connected with evangelization...is in transition or crisis.... This hesitation or even confusion concerning evangelization has not only left a feeling of insecurity in this whole area of the Lord's manifestation to the world; it has weakened and even stifled the missionary spirit which has always characterized the Society" (Allocution of January 6).

Disarray, confusion, and division therefore seem to be standard in the history of the church. Christians have always disagreed about the interpretation of their faith, both practical and theoretical. They have always struggled to clarify what God was asking of them. Little about God is obvious or undebatable. Little about human beings is uniform and unchanging. So when we take up the question of what the church might be, were Christians to realize their full potential, we ought to do so with a smile. The word *might* tells us that we are involved with what Albert Einstein called a "thought experiment." As Einstein's own career shows, thought experiments can be immensely valuable. However, they never remove the messiness of the actual world. Historically and politically, the church is much more than a thought experiment or even a thought experiment carried out by God. We do best when we accept this situation with good humor, not taking ourselves too seriously. We Christians are the clowns of God, the certain screwups. God must be patient with us, able to preserve a twinkle in her eye.

Such a twinkle does not mean that there is no place for tears, either in God's eye or our own. The people of God have suffered great pain, much of it of their own making. Indeed, they have inflicted great pain on non-Christians, for which God has to call them to judgment. Our disarray has been moral as well as political and intellectual. We have verified Paul's lament, not doing the good that we wanted to do and doing the evil that we did not want to do. In a word, we have been sinful, again and again choosing against God and our own best interests. That is the hallmark of sin: an intrinsic irrationality. How could his countrymen have rejected Jesus, whom Christians consider God's greatest gift? How could East and West have split over relatively trivial doctrinal and disciplinary matters? How could Catholics and Protestants have refused to compromise even when they could see that they were destroying Christ's work? There are no good answers to questions such as these, and our own examinations of conscience show us why. We cannot explain the sin in our own lives, because it is irrational. We do not know why we can become blind and forget what is important.

This applies in the matter of ecumenism. Nowadays the Christian churches have mostly settled back into their divisions, accepting separation as simply the way that things are. After a flurry of enthusiasm for reunification that reached a high water mark during the Second Vatican Council (1962–65), Protestants, Catholics, and Orthodox have tacitly agreed that there is no imperative to drop their different organizational structures and rework themselves into one great church. Certainly, their theologians have made significant progress through many-sided discussions, but those holding power have not used this theological progress to work out imaginative paths to actual merger. So while it is a blessing that few groups still hate one another as they did fifty years ago, it is a scandal that the will to heal the battered body of Christ has proved to be so tepid.

In the next section, I shall reflect on the freedom available in thought experiments about what the church could be. There the topic will be what the word *ideal* in my title can mean. Here let me anticipate that freedom by musing about a traditional maxim that came into renewed prominence a generation ago because it was a favorite of Pope John XXIII. The maxim says, "In necessary things, unity; in doubtful things, liberty; and in all things, charity." When I consider the disarray of the Christian community, both past and present, it seems obvious that most things are doubtful. From convictions about church order (forms of government) to convictions about homosexuality, a great deal is disputed, debated, controverted. The traditional maxim suggests that in a state of affairs such as this, liberty ought to prevail. Until matters sort themselves out, people ought to be free to work experimentally, following their consciences and offering one another kindly criticism.

My own view is that necessary things are few yet utterly important. I cannot conceive of a Christian church worthy of the name that did not subscribe to the traditional (for instance, Nicene) creed. In the moral realm, I cannot conceive of jettisoning the ten commandments of Moses or the twofold commandment of Christ. In the realm of worship, I find word and sacrament essential to the constitution of the church as a body of orthodox (healthy) believers. But beyond these bare bones, this necessary skeleton, most other matters admit of some flexibility. For example, the history of doctrine suggests that whether there are seven sacraments or two is less important than the conviction that Jesus left his community a tradition of breaking bread in memory of him. Similarly, it suggests that whether the community ought to have an episcopal or a presbyterian or a congregational form of government is less important than the conviction that it ought to have leaders equipped to keep it in good order. When Augustine uttered his famous line, "Love and do what you will," he was moving in the direction that I am sketching here. He did not mean that all courses of action were equally good, that no criticism was necessary. He meant that the key to right Christian behavior is love like that shown by Christ. He was reminding his hearers that without love we are likely to get lost in accidentals.

We are bound to the few essentials, the skeletal necessities like the creed, for without them we cannot be the community of Christ. Without them we do not know who we are or what we ought to be doing. And we are bound to try to make these essential elements of our faith shape how we think about other matters, such as how we behave and how we pray. But if we commit ourselves to the creed, to worship through word and sacrament, and to behavior (political, economic, sexual) that is loving, we can work out the rest well enough to be the community that Jesus intended. Our disarray will be more the untidiness inevitable for diverse, changing people than the untidiness caused by culpable ignorance, willful sin. I believe that thought experiments, forays into ideal thinking, can help us to see this distinction clearly. There is disarray and disarray—one kind right and the other kind wrong. Happy are we when we know the difference.

But, you may say, Christians have also debated about the creed, about proper worship, and about love. True, so they have. However, I think that an ecumenical, catholic consensus has emerged historically to offer enough light to guide our way in all three areas. Since the councils of Nicaea (325) and Chalcedon (451), the main lines of the key Christian doctrines have been clear. The confession in the mainstream has been that God is a community of three unlimited "persons" who share one divine nature, and that Jesus the Christ is one divine "person" with two full natures (human and divine). This confession gave voice to what a majority of the fourth and fifth century conciliar bishops thought had been latent in Christian discipleship from the beginning and offered the best interpretation of the

9

Christian scriptures (by that time the New Testament was virtually intact). Certainly, the positions of Christians with reservations about some of these formulations, such as the Arians, require serious consideration, but in retrospect their deviation from what the orthodox now consider the mainstream was relatively slight.

One can make a parallel analysis about the differences between Eastern and Western Christians in the eleventh century and between Protestants and Catholics in the sixteenth century. They held much more in common (doctrinally, liturgically, and ethically) than they held apart. Their tragedy was that they could not love the common more than the particular, the good of the whole more than the good of their part. Today, in the broader perspective offered by the full span of the world religions, one can only weep at their narrowness. Like the Jerusalem over which Jesus wept, they did not know the things for their peace. The sobering reality, however, is that we, their latter-day descendants, have maintained much of their ignorance. We could be a much healthier body of Christ if we would accept a commonsensical view of the few essentials, grant one another wide liberty concerning the many doubtful things, and in all things make love our badge of honor.

I have suggested the benefit of stepping back from the actual or historical to imagine the ideal. Let me develop this suggestion. A thought-experiment is a free zone, where we let ourselves prescind from the lets and hindrances that can stifle our creativity. Certainly, we ought never to lose sight of the constraints under which any plan will labor when we try to put it into practice. But by declaring a free zone we can inoculate ourselves against the cynicism and discouragement that too-close attention to such constraints can engender. It may well be that our ideal view of the church will become platonic, something that we have to use as an inspiration more than a template. But usually we will be the better for having raised our sights, having let our fancy run free. In the case of theology, our fancy can be driven by faith, hope, and love—the theological virtues that the Spirit of Christ pours forth in our spirits. We can find our courage rising, our discouragement abating, because the Spirit can use our imaginative work to remind us that nothing is impossible with God. Jesus said that faith can move mountains. We need to remember this saying regularly.

When Pope John XXIII had his vision of bringing the church up to date, he came under the influence of what I am calling an ideal. His vision led to the Second Vatican Council, which today we can judge to have been only a partial success. Nonetheless, the Council was the most energizing moment in the twentieth century of Christian history, and without it there is no telling how far Roman Catholicism, if not the Christian community as a whole, might have fallen out of touch with the contemporary world. Like any reformation or revolution, the Council set in motion forces that church leaders proved unable to control. It raised hopes that they could not fulfill. But it was an authentic gathering of Christian leaders, and on their own terms even conservative Catholic Christians are bound to respect the work of the Holy Spirit within it. So the thought-experiment of Pope John XXIII continues to bear significant fruits. Despite all the difficulties of working out its full implications, his contemplation of a new ideal has changed the face of the church for the better.

Our goal has to be incomparably more modest, of course, but the same dynamics are at work. Inasmuch as we are embarking on a time of creative musing, even dreaming, we too cannot be sure what the consequences will be. So we have to persuade ourselves that the musing itself is beneficial, regardless of whether or not what we envision ever comes to pass. We have to believe that our journeys through the free zone, the no-place (utopia) of faith, can be their own reward. We have no right to forget that sin and legitimate differences of opinion are certain to dog any practical projects that idealistic theologizing brings to trial. But we do have the right to let the logic of our musing move ahead without hindrance from premature worries about sin and other sources of difficulty. We can say that freeing people's minds and hearts sufficiently to let them entertain putting our new possibilities into practice is not our responsibility but that of the Holy Spirit. We may point to the reception of Pope John XXIII's dream as an encouraging sign that the Spirit does her part. And we can even promise ourselves that working at our thought-experiment will bring us closer to the Spirit, because it will draw forth our best intuitions of what God wants, how God moves the church forward, and which ways are the ways of God.

In Bernard Lonergan's analysis of redemption, the work of Christ proceeds by "the law of the cross." What Jesus does in forgiving his enemies is to break the cycle of tit for tat. Loving his enemies, he takes away the energy that keeps our normal antagonisms going. His enemies expect him to stand at the accustomed distance and trade blow for blow. By moving in to embrace them, he frustrates their expectation. He absorbs their blows without returning any of his own, and the best of them realize that this takes away their basis for anger. They cannot continue to hate him because he does them no injury. Certainly, the enemies who are worst remain beyond the reach of his goodness, but this only makes their wrongness more plain. Jesus is not trying to accuse them, but the effect of his love is to bring them under a sentence of God that declares them to be hateful sinners.

We may never become martyrs like Jesus, witnesses unto blood, but perhaps we can become better disciples and peacemakers. Perhaps musing about what Jesus has done, how the law of the cross works redemptively, can give us new tools for improving our situations at work, in our families, wherever antagonism rages. Musing is common to creative people. Good bosses and mothers muse about problems at work or in the family circle, as good artists muse about problems with their paintings and good scientists muse about problems with their experiments. Experience shows that creativity of this sort has to be free, in the sense of not pressured unduly to produce immediate results. It depends on moving outside customary assumptions, finding breaks in the stone walls, and so access to new pastures. So creative musing can take us to the door of the inner chapel, inviting us in to pray. Some species of contemplative prayer amount to little more than appreciating the endlessness of God's own creativity and goodness. We can do worse on our knees than simply thanking God for being God—always being greater than our creaturehood.

That God is God is our best, finally our only, hope for redemption, salvation, or making progress toward the kind of church that God deserves. With God there are no dead ends. Agreed, we can only keep this faith through God's own grace. But a great cloud of saintly witnesses encourages us to go along, day by day, praying for such maintenance. Often, I try to remember how central the passover of Jesus is to my faith. If Christ is not risen, Paul said, our faith is in vain. Since Christ is risen, we too may rise, and the mere possibility of this rising detonates the prison in which unbelief would keep me. Ideally, I would always live outside the prison of unbelief, a free spirit empowered by the resurrection of Christ. Actually, I spend a great deal of time behind bars, a practical atheist. So it is a boon to meditate again about the foundations of my existence, the difference that a living faith can make. Once again, I can experience a liberation, as my horizon expands and the chains to which I have submitted fall away.

For this book, my hope is that author and reader alike can experience again some of the liberation that Christian discipleship can bring. By musing together about what the community of Christ could be, were we all thorough believers, perhaps we can both come away the stronger. For the possibilities are dazzling; nothing less than complete human fulfillment.

MARKS: OLD AND NEW

The church itself has sometimes been idealistic, raising its gaze above the hurly-burly of its actual, empirical existence to remind itself of what it is more substantially in the creative design of God. The traditional marks of the church express this idealism. In substance, according to the creative design of God, the Christian community is one, holy, catholic, and apostolic. Regardless of its fracture and sin, its provincialism and historical change, the church has always managed to be these good things for people of faith—people willing to grant it the prejudices of love. Let us use these four traditional marks to advance our sense of what an ideal ecclesiology entails.

ONE. What makes the community of Christ one—sufficiently united to claim the identity that its function in the economy of salvation requires? In the final analysis, the commission of the Father resulting in the work of Jesus and his Spirit is the source of Christian unity. The prayer of Jesus recorded in John 17 symbolizes how the early Christians regarded the basis for Christian unity. Jesus wanted his community to reflect the unity that he enjoyed with his heavenly Father. Moreover, the unity of his followers was to be the great sign to the world that the Father had sent Jesus as the way to salvation. So the unity of the church is different from that to which a political party or even a family of blood relations may aspire. The unity of the church rests on the will and action of God, who wants to make the followers of Jesus a sign of what love can do when it sets no limits to what the divine Spirit may make of it.

Because God gives the church its crucial unity, the church can never fail to be one. When we muse about this implication, we find many hopeful possibilities. For example, beneath our divisions as Protestants, Catholics, and Orthodox, we Christians share a more significant unity. Inasmuch as we confess the same Lord and enjoy the same Spirit, we are far more alike than different. Our tendency has been and is to forget this greater likeness and concentrate on our lesser differences: relatively small points of doctrine or liturgical practice or church polity. If we could focus less on our shabby selves, or on the injuries we think that others have inflicted on us, and more on the majesty of God, we could shame ourselves into forgetting most of our grievances.

Another encouraging implication of the substantial unity that God herself gives to us as church is the openendedness of our future. We can make sense of the article of faith concerning the "communion of saints" if we locate sanctity in the gifts of God rather than the achievements of human beings. For then sanctity comes ipso facto from God's presence in us, and sanctity can perdure as long as this presence does. We shall continue to be the disciples of Christ throughout eternity. In history, before eternity, we enjoy a communion with those who have gone before us in faith, again because of the unity that God herself produces. To live in the grace of Christ, in the love that Christ and the Spirit pour forth in our hearts, is to live with all the others who have enjoyed this grace and love. So Peter and Paul, the Blessed Virgin and the Magdalene, Ignatius and Archbishops Bernardin and Romero, Monica and the martyrs of Latin America, your loved ones and mine—the whole roster of saints—becomes our genealogy. As a traditional Chinese family recalls the ancestors who passed on from life, so we Christians call the roll of exemplary forebears who kept the torch burning. A symbolic action, certainly, but also an acknowledgment of the constant work of the Holy Spirit that preserves the Christian community.

A third implication of the substantial unity that the Paraclete gives to the church is that many more people may belong to the community of Christ than show up for overt church activities.

Working in the consciences of all people, the Spirit of Christ may knit together Muslims and Jews, Hindus and unbelievers, overt Christians and arctic shamans, making a communion of saints that escapes the labels and confines that we, in our inevitable narrowness, tend to impose. Clearly, faithful followers of Jesus of Nazareth never fail to appreciate the benefits, even the necessities, of adhering to the historical gospel that he preached and serving it generously in their own day. Assuredly, Pope John Paul II is right to think of the beginning of the third millennium as a natural time for renewing our dedication to evangelization. But it is also true that evangelization, church membership, salvation, and eternal life are works of God more than works of our own. Therefore, we cannot define the boundaries of those works. We cannot say with certitude who hears the gospel successfully, who is a member of the community of Christ, who is saved, what the population of heaven is and is not. These are mysteries because they depend on God more than ourselves and the goodness of God is intrinsically mysterious.

When it comes to the sources of unity that are more human, less profoundly dependent on the action of the Spirit of Christ in our depths, the few necessary things that the church developed relatively early in its history are instructive. We have mentioned the creed (though there were

19

several early versions, they differed from one another only slightly) and the New Testament (which has always served as *the* collection of writings that the church has considered canonical—regulative expressions of faith). We can also mention authoritative leaders descended from the apostles and a regular public worship (one constrained by tradition and authoritative church leaders). These four sources of unity have not been straitjackets, but they have been disciplines, constraints. When various gnostic groups proposed novel interpretations of faith, the proto creeds, scriptures, church authorities, and liturgical disciplines were invoked to rebut them.

I believe that one can legitimately read church history so as to describe a creedal faith, an understanding of Christian scripture, an agreement about church leadership, and a consensus about orthodox worship that is sufficiently consistent and perceptible to delineate a mainstream that would capture 80 percent of Christians. (This judgment only gets stronger if one places the discussion in the context of the world religions or of world history as a whole. Then the differences between episcopal and congregational models of polity, or between churches that celebrate the Lord's supper rarely and those that celebrate it regularly seem small indeed.)

The point is that the traditional mark of oneness is not ideal in a subversive or illusory sense.

It is ideal in the sense that it springs directly from what God has made the church to be and how God has guided the development of the church historically. We should indeed lament the strife that has torn the Christian community apart in past ages, as we should lament the foot-dragging today that keeps present church leaders from responding more effectively to the manifest will of Christ that his community be one visibly, before the world. But we should not let our lamentation blind us to the unity that we already have from a bare confession of faith in Jesus and a simple enjoyment of the life given by his Spirit. We *are* one, and the more fully we appreciate this reality, the easier it will be for us to overcome our pernicious differences, because in contrast they will seem embarrassingly trivial.

HOLY. The second mark of the church that has developed from ideal reflections expresses its sanctity. The community of Christ has sufficient unity with its Lord to make it partake of his sanctity. Sanctity, holiness, is a matter of being. From holy being flow holy, saintly actions. The miracles of Jesus were signs of his status as the emissary of God, "the bringer of salvation." The ultimate expression of Jesus' holy being was his dying on the cross in fidelity to his mission. Thus the centurion whom Mark uses as an objective witness confesses that Jesus truly was the son of God. The implication that Mark wants to drive home is that the way that Jesus died was so extraordinary that he must have been extraordinarily close to God.

We Western Christians tend to overlook the ontological dimension of our church membership. We are not accustomed to thinking about what flows from our being united to Christ through faith. The most significant thing about any believer is the share in holy, deathless life that faith brings. This most significant thing does not work at odds with the individual traits that make each of us who we are. Closeness to God, intensity of sharing divine life, makes us more ourselves, not less. But we modern Westerners are so oriented to activity that often we fail to appreciate that grace changes what we are. For example, as human, we are mortal. As sinful, we are disordered. The life of God in us draws us into the immortality of the divine. Equally, it draws us into the holiness of God. Certainly, we have a role to play in the flourishing of this life. We have to say yes to the initiatives of the Spirit and agree to the ascetic demands that faith imposes. We have to want the goodness of God more than any passing goods and so let our submission to death become a gentle subversiveness of our mortality. The articles of the creed that affirm the resurrection of the body and the life of the world to come assume that we are agreeing to the transforming work of the Spirit in our core being.

Just as the flesh of Jesus became the basic sacrament of God's love, so our flesh can serve as a fundamental sign that the reign of God is not an illusion but a present, powerful reality. In modest measure, we can keep present in the world the striking goodness that leads people to believe that God cares for them. Such striking goodness is what people mean when they called Mother Teresa of Calcutta, or Dorothy Day, or the Mahatma Gandhi a saint. Something lucid, unusually real and winning, shines from such people. They have realized what in the rest of us remains only potential. By some combination of God's gift and their own response, they have whittled away the egocentricity that keeps the rest of us from being similarly transparent, integral, real.

If you read the advice of elders to youngsters, whether they are classical Romans or pre-Columbian Aztecs, you find the theme that the company one keeps is important. Life in the community of Christ ought to furnish us with good example, friends sharing our journey and helping us along. There ought to be a positive contagion, so that living well becomes the thing to do. Often I think that our churches aim too low. We could do more to instruct our people that they have holiness in their depths as a right, a reality. Through baptism they have entered on the life of God, which is always holy. Yes, they have to pray and dedicate themselves to improving the welfare of their neighbors, but these obligations quickly lose their burdensomeness and become congenial. We realize that holiness is less a matter of exceptional deeds than of doing well—conscientiously, kindly, steadily—the ordinary tasks that our responsibilities entail.

Thousands of nurses, mothers, fathers, clerks, college presidents, postal workers, and others do this each day. They put aside what they might prefer, were they free to consult only their own preferences, and do what has to be done if they are to love their neighbors as themselves. Whether they pray similarly effectively is hard to determine, because prayer is often private. But most Christians raise their minds and hearts to God regularly—a quick petition here, a nighttime "thanks" there. Many would be embarrassed to say how they pray, but pray they do, keeping a lifeline open. They want to be connected with God, even when they are not sure what "God" means. They would like to do God's will, but often it seems obscure. Would stressing the holiness that comes from plain faith help them appreciate better what is going on? Perhaps. The truth is that God is most of our being and salvation. The theological fact is that God wants to give us an ever fuller share of divine life and holiness. To say that God is the primary partner in our enterprise is to make the entire enterprise completely hopeful. Thus, saying "thy will be done" can be a cry of liberation.

Holiness comes from the triumph of God's will for us, which is our prospering. Yes, God's view of "prospering" may differ from ours, as the example of Jesus shows. But this should not lead us to suspect pleasure or good times. After all, one of Jesus' figures for heaven is a messianic banquet—a great party. Nor should the obscurity of God's understanding of prospering make us expect holiness to be painful. In itself, the life of God is effortless—full of grace, lithe and easy. Pain comes from the limits and sins that we run up against, both outside and in our own consciences. But we should avoid the paranoia that expects trouble around every corner. Sufficient for the day is the evil thereof. When pain comes, we have to trust that God will see us through. God's seeing us through does not mean that the pain will go away. That may happen or it may not. But regardless of what happens, we have an assurance bred into our faith that God never abandons us, always continues to care for our well-being.

Even in extremis, we are right to cling to this assurance, as Jesus did on the cross. He thought that God would take better care of him than he could. And on the other side of his dying, in the strange but decisive experience that we call the resurrection, God did take complete care of him. The resurrection was the ratification of all that

Jesus had done, God's complete seal of approval. The good implication for our reflections on the holiness of the church is that the triumph of Jesus is our own. In virtue of him, we can hope to gain a complete union with God beyond the limits imposed by our flesh. What is present now in our depths will flower then like an Easter bouquet.

CATHOLIC. One and holy, the church is also catholic—universal. In principle, the community of Christ extends to every corner of the earth, every tribe and epoch. The decision for this universality came early, when the apostles sanctioned Paul's mission to the gentiles. The New Testament witnesses that from its first generations the church understood its membership to be open to all who wanted to join. Catholicity is the effect of this understanding.

For most of its history the church did not have to think deeply about such catholicity. Karl Rahner has divided church history into three periods. The first was the brief time when the church of the apostles was largely a Jewish Christian enclave. By the end of the first century, however, the church had embarked on an expansion that eventually made it the major religious institution in Europe. With colonialism, the church also became the major religious institution in North America, Latin America, and Australia, as well as a significant factor in Africa and India. Now, in a third period, when history has become truly global, Rahner sees the need for the church to look critically at its Eurocentrism and to explore more boldly the catholicity present at its core.

In principle, there is no reason why the church should be more Italian or French than Nigerian or Peruvian. Certainly, the church will always reflect its original Jewish and Greek cultural foundations. As well, it will always be wise to study the given history that it has developed, which centers in Europe. But among the necessary things on which all Christians have to agree I do not find a European mentality. The Christian theology that has developed owes a great deal to European culture, and there is no reason to deprecate this heritage. Equally, however, there is no reason to consider it chiseled in stone or having to be replicated everywhere on earth. Yes, it is a delicate task to determine what is extricable from a given formulation of orthodox faith, morals, or worship and what is not, but this is a task that competent theologians and pastors can carry out adequately. The main thing to secure is the right of the church to adapt its formulations to changing historical and cultural situations. Catholicity is a good peg on which to hang this right. Because the church has the mission to preach the good news to the ends of the earth, it has the right to adapt this preaching as it finds necessary.

How ought the church to engage in this process? By trial and error, with full dialogue. The only way to determine whether a given liturgical form works in Africa or Latin America or India is to try it. Full discussion beforehand should insure that those designing the form understand what is to be communicated. There is no question, for example, of ignoring or diluting the full humanity and divinity of Jesus. But there are dozens of ways that one can celebrate this central doctrine. Similarly, it is constitutive of the eucharist that it be both a meal and a sacrifice. In remembering what Jesus did with his disciples at his farewell dinner and what he did on the cross, Christians keep present the passover that gave birth to their faith. This has always been the gist of their Sunday assembling. So no rightful adaptation will leave this gist behind. On the other hand, because different ethnic groups celebrate in different ways, the church ought to be flexible about how it works out its eucharistic celebrations.

Catholicity therefore implies trusting local Christians to discern the implications of their faith responsibly. Having instructed them in the fundamentals, church officials ought to trust local Christians to communicate accurately what the fundamentals mean in Guatemala in contrast to Berlin. The basis for this trust is the presence in all believers of the Spirit of Christ, who alone can guarantee orthodoxy. It is desirable for Christians to challenge one another, in love and mutual respect, to minimize aberrations. A sense of what the whole tradition has been and of what the church worldwide is doing can do wonders in this regard. But our challenging of one another ought to be democratic in the sense of being mutual. Each Christian is competent to say what faith has meant in her or his own life.

Beyond this competence, of course, lie the competencies that only come from study, but proper theological study remains throughout *faith* seeking understanding. The faith retains an important priority. The community is the richer for having all its members involved in the project of working out what its faith ought to mean in a given situation. It suffers when a few "experts" at the top hand down to the "simple faithful" at the bottom what such and such an article of faith means or how the community ought to conduct such and such an item of business. John Henry Newman raised this commonsense observation to the level of a theological principle by elaborating the need for "consulting the faithful in matters of doctrine." His point was that the Spirit of God working in all believers' hearts inspires a rich variety of insights that church leaders neglect at their peril.

Clearly, the catholicity in question here is not the exclusive property of Roman Catholics. Protestants and Orthodox are as much held to catholicity as are Roman Catholics. Their sense of the church is equally universal. In fact, a sectarian Christianity, limited to a particular ethnic group or to those who adhere to marginal doctrines, is a contradiction in terms. The church cannot be the community of Christ in a mental cul-de-sac. It has to reach out to the whole world, offering the good news to all with ears to hear. In necessary things, unity—but only in truly necessary things. Beyond the creed, each doctrinal requirement ought to be pressured to make its case—show why all believers should be held to it.

A similar minimalism that would allow people to adapt their ethical practices and worship as in conscience they find best could give further flesh to the mark of catholicity. The church ought to celebrate diversity, when it comes from solid prayer and religious instinct. This does not mean overthrowing the ten commandments, nor giving carte blanche in the area of euthanasia or abortion. It does not mean that a given community does not need to establish stringent criteria for admission to orders. But it does mean that the church ought to want fully honest discussions of any pressing issue: abortion, the ordination of women, physician-assisted suicide, cloning, genetic engineering. It does mean that consulting the faithful in these matters is an obvious way to express catholicity.

When Christians come together, they ought not to be proponents of "multiculturalism," in the recent ideological use of this term. Their gatherings ought not to be political occasions when they plump for the cultural riches of their own particular ethnic heritage. Christians come together in their most characteristic, constitutive assembling to celebrate their common faith in the Lordship of Jesus, their common joy at the salvation that their Lord offers them. If rightly ordered, a Christian assembly focuses more on God than on the human participants. In the process of celebrating this common faith and joy, the people may indeed draw on their particular cultural heritages. Indeed, they are bound to do so, if their celebrations are to be gripping. But a sense of proportion should keep their focus on God primary. It is true enough that God is only God for us in our concrete circumstances. It is also true that only God makes those concrete circumstances salvific.

When church leaders find groups apparently ignoring this sense of proportion, they are right to offer corrections. They should do this, however, in intimate exchanges with such groups. It is foolish to try to make corrections from a distance, without close knowledge of the particular circumstances involved. If acquiring such knowledge requires invoking the principle of subsidiarity, which tells us that we should try to solve problems at the most local level possible, so much the better. What should not happen is that church leaders devalue their authority by pontificating from afar. They are dealing with matters of conscience, which are irreducibly personal. This is not to say that there are no general principles at work in a healthy Christian ethics or liturgical practice. It is simply to invoke the long tradition, adapted by Christians from classical Greek philosophy, that prudence has to mediate between general principles and particular circumstances.

Without prudence, people trying to apply ethical or liturgical principles are bound to be ineffective—wooden, if not legalistic. And, in Christian perspective, the natural virtue of prudence folds into the wisdom that is a gift of the Holy Spirit. As people mature in their faith, they gain from the Spirit a connatural sense of what befits their Christian profession and what does not. They know, intuitively, that celebrating the eucharist with a Danish pastry is not fitting. Equally, they know that they cannot hold any human life cheap, expendable. So after they have listened to the technical data about the use of fetal tissue in therapies for Parkinson's disease, they must sit back to sift it through a Christian sense of what is right. In addition, they should tend to raise further questions: Where does this fetal tissue come from? Is it the result of abortions? Were the abortions carried out for the purpose of securing the tissue? What impact would employing such tissue probably have on most citizens' reverence for human life?

This is how the Spirit works in live Christian consciences. When we are not disquieted, made uneasy by a proposal, we can move to carry it peacefully. When we are disquieted, we ought to pause to discover why. Because this capacity to pause and discover why we are disquieted is found wherever the Spirit of Christ is present, we can call it *catholic.* If we extend this principle to the ecumene, the wide world in which the church labors today, we find that catholicity entails making dialogue a regular way of Christian discernment.

APOSTOLIC. The fourth mark of the church, as idealistic reflection loves to contemplate it, is its constitutive tie to the first followers of Jesus, those who knew him in the flesh and were eye-witnesses to his work, death, and resurrection. Christian tradition considers these apostles its anchor. What church officials, theologians, and ordinary parents hand down generation after generation is rooted in the very beginnings of the community. The New Testament sprang from the apostolic witness to what Jesus had been, said, done, and suffered. The developments that new problems required led the faithful back to their apostolic foundation, so that they might feel sure that their adaptations were wise. There is no other rightful foundation than that which Jesus laid down and the first generation of his followers secured. People who deviated from this foundation were heretics or schismatics. As centers of apostolic tradition, the church soon established Rome, Antioch, Jerusalem, Alexandria, and Constantinople. They were patriarchal centers, revered for the flourishing of faith that had occurred in their areas. Gradually Rome gained a primacy, largely because (a) it was considered the center of the imperial world in which the church lived and (b) it earned a reputation for having the purest doctrinal tradition.

When the empire established Constantinople as a second, Eastern Rome, the differentiation of the church into Latin-speaking and Greek-speaking zones advanced markedly. Later, when Eastern Orthodoxy spread to the Slavs and Constantinople lay under Muslim dominance, Moscow advertised itself as a third Rome, but on the whole Moscow did not gain standing equal with Italian Rome and Constantinople. Antioch continued to be the center of Syriac Christian traditions, while Geneva could lay some claim to being the center of the Protestant church world (though the autonomy that most Protestant groups sought rendered the notion of a directive center suspect).

In recent ecumenical discussions among the three major historical branches of Christianity, the Petrine ministry embodied in the bishop of Rome has emerged as a signal source for the unity of the church as a whole. The tradition that both Peter and Paul died in Rome gives Rome a strong claim to primacy in matters apostolic, while the monarchical character of Roman Catholic polity has the advantage of making its source of authority the simplest and clearest. How the pope ought to function in the twenty-first century as a center of church unity remains undetermined. The willingness of some Anglicans and Lutherans to take seriously the primacy of Peter over the church ecumenical is a fine sign for the ecumenical future. However, the failure of the Vatican to act creatively in response to this good will has been a damper. Still, in the measure that it prizes apostolicity, any Christian community is primed to want the most effective link possible to the foundations that the church de facto built for itself. One cannot responsibly separate the New Testament aspects of these foundations from the apostolic, so in the measure that a community is evangelical it has to grapple with the issue of how it is honoring apostolicity.

Related to apostolicity is also the matter of church order. If it is to be one substantially, beneath its considerable disarray on the surface, the community of Christ has to be a place of peace and concord. It cannot make antagonism, dysfunction, or confusion into business as usual, the order of the day. It has to establish sufficient orderliness to show that it remains the unified community that Jesus founded and for which he prayed in the Johannine version of his final preparation for his passion. Order is not uniformity, making all soldiers march in lockstep. It can love variety, diversity, local color. But in necessary things, unity—and so order. Even in doubtful things, where liberty ought to prevail, there is no justification for license.

A healthy church shows its good order by balancing self-concern with concern for the outside world. It is true that the church does not exist for itself, inasmuch as evangelization is essential to its vitality. It is also true that judgment begins with the house of God, in the sense that unless the church has its own affairs in order it will only spread disorder when evangelizing outsiders. Similarly, a healthy church walks a fine line between reverence for tradition and openness to the signs of new times. It is neither overly conservative nor overly innovative. It makes haste slowly, but it avoids stasis. It rejects the motto of Cardinal Ottaviani, *Semper Idem* (Always the Same), but it sympathizes with his intent.

Where does the church get such balance?

Ultimately, only from the Spirit who gives it its substantial oneness and holiness. However, in more proximate, apparently human terms, regular dialogue and the ministry of orders come to mind. Unless the church universal is a community of constant conversation, peaceful buzz day and night about the welfare of what all healthy members love dearly, it will not accomplish the orderly change, the measured development, that God's having established it in history requires. The ministry of orders, which sets aside leaders charged to oversee the maintenance of good order in the church, has a crucial role in such development.

Orders is a charism from the Spirit of Christ based on God's call to abide in the life of the Father, Son, and Spirit. Since such abiding cannot be static, the community must practice an ongoing discernment that enables it to determine prudently which proposed courses of action hold the best promise for bringing the church forward desirably. It must also practice an ongoing critique of what past choices have wrought, so as to avoid repeating mistakes and to capitalize on strategies that have turned out well. These processes require supervision, through both initiative and oversight. They also require judgments that bring the ongoing dialogue, discernment, and criticism to term, when they have obviously reached a natural climax or when practical action is imperative.

Those holding office in the community of Christ ought to enjoy the support of the communities that they are leading. Whatever is the constituency that a given leader guides, it ought to have had a significant say in his or her selection, and so, good confidence that the person selected is well suited for the job. The person ought to be wise in the ways of Christ, well schooled and experienced. She or he ought also to be a model of discipleship and someone skilled at bringing out the best in other people. A balance between listening carefully to the reports of all the members of the group, so as to know what their experience suggests, and being able to make crisp decisions when the proper time has come, marks all effective leadership in the church.

Christian leadership cannot be arbitrary, and it ought not to be ill-informed. It ought to be humble, taking to heart the notion that a Christian leader is a servant of the servants of God. The main reason for leadership is simply the good living of Christian life. Orders are not an end in themselves, a sacral rank in a great chain of being. So questions about sex or marital status or sexual orientation, while well worth considering, should be quite secondary to questions about *holiness* (good character, discipline, virtue), *intelligence* (competence, skilled prudence), and *charisma* (personal warmth, leadership) that go to the heart of the task. If the church is to keep faith with its apostolic foundations and honor the instances when it has enjoyed remarkable leadership, we shall have to shake up many current patterns.

ECUMENICAL. When I think of an ideal church for the twenty-first century, it carries "ecumenical" like a fifth, precisely contemporary mark. Yes, much that the marks of unity and catholicity imply covers what the ecumenical movement has tried to restore. But this movement has grappled admirably with the historical divisions that have marred both the being and the witness of the church, bringing many Christians to a deeper awareness of the sinfulness of their past and also of their need for constant reform. As well, it has brought out the values of pluralism, congenial to democratic Americans but still suspect in many parts of the world, including Rome.

For present purposes, I assume that there are three major families of churches within the Christian community: Protestant, Catholic, and Orthodox. Some commentators make the evangelical churches a fourth family, but most such churches owe their origins to Protestantism. The evangelical impulses that have arisen recently in the Catholic camp may rightly claim to be retrieving neglected elements of that tradition, such as taking inspiration from the Spirit and making the Bible the center of spirituality, but in

39

fact Protestant evangelicals have been the stimulus to this retrieval. I know little about evangelical impulses in Orthodoxy, though I have visited a flourishing Baptist church in Moscow. Recent legislation shows that, just as Protestant evangelicals in Latin America have come to worry the Vatican, so too, in the countries of the former Soviet Union they have wrinkled the brows of Orthodox leaders (as have Roman Catholic proselytizers).

When I have thought lately about the basic differences in theological styles that Protestants, Catholics, and Orthodox typically or stereotypically exhibit, I have been encouraged to find them complementary. Momentarily we can consider how to untangle or forgive the history of the rifts among these families of churches, but here let us console ourselves by appreciating one of the positive results of the families' separate developments. In my thinking, Protestants favor a dialectical style keenly aware of the oppositions and negativities at work in the world, faith, and the human mind. Catholics favor an analogical style more at home in the world and more sacramental. Orthodox favor a mystical style that traditionally has seen reality as filled with God's Spirit, and so, has read earthly life typologically, as a pale reflection of heavenly glories.

A dialectical theological style is passionate about the soleness of God. It is, in the phrase of

H. Richard Niebuhr, a radical monotheism. An analogical style draws its energy from the incarnation, thinking that there God has shown the balanced, both/and character of reality, making theology an effort to show how divine things are both like and unlike the best human things. A mystical style is quickly liturgical, loving to celebrate the divine beauty and drawn to the silence that the best song suggests is our purest adoration.

Though in practice the interaction of these different styles can become irritating, in idealistic meditation they seem excellent checks and balances. None of the church families denies the radical monotheism that is the powerhouse of dialectical theology, but the Catholic and Orthodox pieties, with their sumptuous liturgies, ranks of saints, and bevies of icons can seem to underplay it. None of the families denies the incarnation or the sacramentality that flows from it, but the Protestant and Orthodox pieties have not generated the at-home-ness in history that the Catholic analogical style has generated when operating at its best. Similarly, though neither Protestants nor Catholics need deny that the Spirit of the risen Christ so fills creation that human existence is thoroughly pneumatic, the mystical style of the Orthodox brings this out with a clearer invitation to archetypal mysticism than do the others.

Inasmuch as ecumenical progress makes the treasures of each family more available to the others, it holds the potential for a considerable enrichment. As in a good marriage, "mine" and "thine" lose any hard and fast boundaries. Each can contribute according to its gifts and receive according to its needs. Standing in the way of such progress, of course, is the families' legacy of historical divisions. Due to ordinary human inertia and not a small admixture of sinful stubbornness, many members in all three major families have come to accept, even prize, their existence in the part. They have let opposition to the other families in the church universal become part of their self-definition, and they have used it prejudicially to exalt their own kind.

Manifestly, this is contrary to the example of Jesus, who opened his table to all and prayed passionately that all of his people would be one. The disciples of Jesus ought to constitute one flock and have only one shepherd: Jesus himself. It is hard to think of anything wounding the sacred heart of Jesus more than the hatreds that have caused his followers in all three families to become the persecutors, indeed the murderers, of members of other families. The crusades, the inquisitions, the religious wars of the past; today's bloodshed in Northern Ireland and Africa; the rivalries among mainline and fundamentalist Christians; the incivility between liberal and conservative Catholics—these larger and smaller out-bursts of internecine strife understandably have sometimes made the name *"Christian"* odious. How can we redeem this legacy?

Only by forgiving one another. This is far from being as banal a proposition as you may think. Go to the "holy land" today, booking into a hotel in Jerusalem. Talk to Israeli Jews, Palestinian Muslims, and Palestinian Christians. See how kindly a reception your talk about forgiveness receives. A few years ago, when a group of Jewish, Muslim, and Christian scholars to which I belonged discussed this possibility with Israelis and Palestinians, we heard a dozen cautions (which in fact were rejections) for every one invitation to speak on. *Forgiveness* was not exactly a dirty word, but it was a word consigned to the dustbin, the pile of ideas considered irrelevant. Each party had so many grievances on its mind, so many running sores in its soul, that it wanted all your attention to focus on its victimhood. Its was the cause that was righteous. Theirs was the cause that was hateful, violent, irrational, unjust. Our group of scholars had heard all too similar a story when we met in Graz, Austria, only an hour from the war zones of the former Yugoslavia. There the players wore different uniforms—Orthodox Serbs, Catholic Croats, Bosnian Muslims—but forgiveness was equally ridiculed.

So, were the Christian community of the twenty-first century to become effectively ecumenical through a round-robin exercise of forgiveness, it could indeed become the great city raised high on the hill to show the nations what they might be. Hindus and Muslims in India, tribalist peoples all over Africa need such a showing. The hatreds of other Asians for the Japanese, of many Europeans for Germans, and of various economic classes or races for others in countries everywhere are fully relevant. People can become antagonistic, hateful, from their first imbibing of their mother's milk. An ecumenical church that put its own house in order, overcoming its hate-filled past by soul-breaking work to become truly reunited, could offer the bosom of "mother church" as the source of re-creative grace without blushing. Until that day, our preachings to the world will continue to ring hollow, our witness continue to be sterile. Ecumenical reunion is not a luxury. Our division remains our greatest liability and scandal.

CHAPTER 2
THE PEOPLE OF GOD

While the marks pinpoint what constitutes the church, a title like "the people of God" enfleshes it. "The people of God" conjures up images of vast hordes of human beings striving to become what they believe they are. Their goal is nothing less than holiness, union with God. The people of God. Ponder it. Savor it. Let the image flood your imagination. Now, for the next few minutes, permit me to do the same.

I want us to use the roles of laity, religious, priest, bishop, and pope as lenses through which we spy out what it means for us to be holy. Then, I will ruminate on the church's two forms—institutional and charismatic—to discover how these forms might carry the "people of God" to holiness. The limits of space and competence dictate the scope of my musing, as they do yours. For example, I can only speak as a married, now widowed, "cradle" Catholic. Perhaps you speak as a single or gay or alienated or divorced or newly-converted Catholic. (Imagine the wealth our collected speculations could bring to the "people of God.")

LAITY: MARRIED AND SINGLE

In Catholic Christianity, marriage is a sacrament, while in Orthodox Christianity it is sacramental. In Protestant Christianity marriage is a high estate, and lay life generally cedes nothing to the life of consecrated religious. Indeed, when we speak about the "saints" in New Testament terms, we mean all those whom baptism has made holy. Certainly, within a few generations of the death of Jesus, Christians who had died for the faith or given exceptional witness in other ways got their names inscribed on honor rolls. Nonetheless, at the outset the basic instinct was that all Christians are members of Christ, filled with his divine life, so that all Christians have a great dignity.

At the least, faith provided reasons for thinking that life was not senseless, that all sorrows and joys subserved a higher purpose. At its best, faith inspired a community warm and happy—supportive in the best of senses. More often than not, lay Christians have lived in middling circumstances, experiencing neither the worst of persecutions nor the best of possible communities. At all times, however, they have had to contend with small opponents within the community and a great opponent in the world without. The world without, the secular realm contending with God for practical loyalty, has always stood over and against religious people, a worm in their conscience or an obstacle in their path. If it had been easy to render to Caesar what was Caesar's, and to render to God what was God's, Jesus' saying would not have required pondering.

Today the huge counterforce of secularism suggests that the tension shaping lay Christian life is, if anything, more powerful than it was in the past. Instead of kings stressing the importance of violent crusades, we now have large governments assuming that religious faith is a private matter—something quite marginal to the affairs of state that preoccupy their leaders. As well, we have a predominantly atheistic culture among our intellectuals, including our academics. Therefore, it takes considerable sophistication to develop a lay faith, a Christian being-in-the-world, that takes current politics and culture seriously and does well by them.

Married lay Christians have to labor to develop such a sophistication in the midst of sexual and familial commitments. Bracketing the context of a homosexual marriage or the experience of single parents, the milieu for the development of the faith of married Christians is sharing life with a person of the opposite sex, and so, thinking of oneself as an actual or potential parent. This double intimate responsibility (for the welfare of both spouse and children) usually inculcates considerable sobriety about the demands of successful lay living. Married people have to think of their jobs as sources of income upon which their spouses and children depend. They have to think of their work, recreation, and politics as exemplary, because others living with them are bound to take a lesson. Personal existence becomes inherently social. Faith is something that one shares willy-nilly. Not to choose (to go to church, to say grace) is also to choose (to be secular, or not to be overtly religious).

People marry to share their lives—bodies, hearts, minds, possessions, fates. They marry to make new families: raise children, take responsibility for a tiny patch of their generation, nation, and earth. The inclination toward becoming one flesh built into most women and men makes certain not only the continuance of the race but also the constancy of heterosexual interactions. The most basic engine of culture is the friction, both positive and negative, between women and men. Of the three separable zones of social interaction—all male, all female, and male-female—the latter comes closest to determining what our kind is, what our people are. This remains completely true in the church, even though often our theology has not been heterosexual or bisexual in the ideal ways that Paul's description in Galatians 3: 28 postulates. Often we have been male and female in ways that privileged one sex and deprecated the other.

No religion, perhaps no time or culture, has handled sex perfectly, or even well enough to serve as a model for all others. As the story of Adam and Eve becoming aware of their nakedness suggests, heterosexuality is not easy, even though often it can be delightful. The historical development of Christian attitudes toward sex incorporated some Jewish and Hellenistic views that, one can argue, did not square with Christianity's own center in the incarnation. In retrospect, the story takes many twists and turns but the upshot is that just as there is no Christian basis for a Levitical view of the priesthood, according to which sexual activity does not befit those who officiate at the altar, so there is no Christian basis for a gnostic view of the body, according to which some natural, requisite functions are unworthy of the holy God.

The taboos that came into Christianity and nourished themselves there worked to the disparagement of women and sexual intercourse. We continue to suffer from their effects, inasmuch as the inequalities burdening many Christian women still depend on the symbolic power of these taboos (for example, the impact of the blood of menstruation and childbirth). So do many of the confusions and pains surrounding pornography, prostitution, contraception, abortion, divorce, homosexuality, and proper love of children.

There is today a growing appreciation of the need for a conjugal spirituality rooted in, and formative of, the experience of marital love and life. In an ideal church, such a spirituality would insist that the primary intent of the sacrament of matrimony is identical with the primary intent of every sacrament: holiness, union with God. All Christians have the responsibility to contribute to a better, healthier sexual ethics and mores, as all Christians have the right. Speaking honestly, from a faith-filled analysis of their experience, all ought to pitch in to make the church a community standing out for its candor and levelheadedness. Sexual love and children are beautiful—incomparable signs that in creation God has done very good work. Married Christians have the fullest opportunity and obligation to testify to this beauty, praise God for this very good work. Thinking about this, I find it clear that Christian marriage does not exist for itself, anymore than the church as a whole exists for itself. Christian marriage exists as the most elementary form of the Christian community, the most nuclear two or three gathering in Christ's name. The church as a whole exists to show all humans beings how God wants them to live together.

Because of both its nuclear status and its numerical significance, the population of married lay Christians (that is, all but the few married people who are also clerics) ought to be the first concern of the church's ministers. When those holding office in the church think of their responsibilities *ad intra* (to their fellow-Christians, as contrasted with children of God outside the ecclesiastical fold), they ought to think of this large bloc of married people. If they did, they would make it their first responsibility to provide eucharistic assemblies where the crucial nourishment of Christian faith occurred through excellent preaching and moving sacramental celebrations. Fine further programs are desirable, but the weekly eucharistic liturgy ought to take as its first audience ordinary lay Christians.

If married Christians do not find the realities of faith with which they deal every day clarified and rendered practicable at the weekly eucharistic assembly of their community, their community is ailing mortally. If they get no help interpreting the lamentable facts that more than half of the marriages in contemporary America end in divorce and only a minority of children grow up in two-parent households, then who can blame them for writing the church off? A mortally ailing, dysfunctional church is any one in which the word does not reverberate powerfully and relevantly, the people do not share the Lord's supper joyously, and so neither prayer nor social action pours forth to give God what is God's, give Caesar what is Caesar's.

Baptism and the eucharist empower ordinary Christians to follow the layman Jesus in working in the world. For married laypeople, the dimension of raising children can be central. For single laypeople, work (sometimes for children) tends to stand out. The differences between the two lay situations are fluid, inasmuch as single people may become married and married people may become single, through divorce or widowhood. It is also fluid inasmuch as single and married people may be doing the same work, collaborating at the same tasks in business or institutional church life. What unites married and single people as laity, however, is their control of their own money, sexuality, and personal freedom.

Let us begin by considering wealth, one product of work in the world. Jesus orients Christian reflection about wealth skeptically. It is easier for a camel to pass through the eye of a needle than for a rich person to enter the kingdom of God. Hyperbolic as the expression is, it gets our attention. Inasmuch as they are comfortable, rich people can forget their radical dependence on God more easily than can poor people. However, often they can also help their neighbors more easily. So wealth is a two-edged sword (especially for people who do not have large family obligations).

Moreover, in most cultures wealth is a path to high social status. The wealthy can command the services of other people and through them work their will. This gives them clout and gains them attention. Many other people either want to benefit from such clout or find themselves ducking so as not to get belted by it. Inasmuch as status and power of this sort tempt any possessor to pride, wealth is problematic on a second score. Indeed, in the catalogues of vices developed by the early Christians who went out to the desert to pursue perfection, greed and pride stand out as capital sins. Inasmuch as wealth becomes allied with such sins, it becomes a more formidable enemy of holiness.

The majority of laypeople are not wealthy, of course, and those who are can find in the traditional manuals of Christian counsel a quick antidote to the dangers of riches: almsgiving. If people use their wealth for the common good as much as for their own pleasure or aggrandizement, they can turn a potential enemy into a friend. The Jewish tradition of good deeds that Jesus inherited thought this way. Indeed, Jesus himself benefited from the support of people with sufficient means to provide him food and lodging. The early Christian movement depended on material benefactors, as have most of the charitable institutions—for example, schools and hospitals—that have proliferated in Christian history.

Recalling that the Hebrew Bible says that God looks on creation as good, we have to think that in itself material plenty is not evil or dirty but a blessing. No more than food or sex is clothing or housing tainted. But common observation of the ways of the rich, in league with the New Testament's descriptions of how Jesus himself lived, tend to write serious Christians a thin material profile.

Concerning sexual activity, the New Testament has Jesus not marrying or being engaged romantically. However, it gives no indication that Jesus denigrated either marriage or romance. Indeed, both his presence at the wedding feast in Cana and the whole slant of his Jewish culture make such a denigration implausible. Still, it seems clear that Jesus found his mission to preach the kingdom of God all-consuming. For that reason, he neither worked at a steady job nor took on a wife and children. The married people whom he called as disciples soon learned that he expected the kingdom to dominate their hearts. This does not mean that we have to take the harshest interpretation of the sayings of Jesus about selling one's goods, leaving father and mother, or letting the dead bury their dead. It does mean that we have to respect the fact that Jesus limited the rights of worldly business, blood ties, and local loyalties.

Jesus pays sexual activity itself little attention.

The Johannine Jesus deals matter-of-factly with the Samaritan woman and (in some manuscripts) the woman caught in adultery. Sexual activity is a fact of life, one of many good things that can be abused. When people do abuse it, not acting in accord with the purposes of God or the holy treasure of divine life dwelling in them, they have to repent and change their ways. When they use sex well, their activity redounds to the praise of their Creator. It is God who has commanded us to increase and multiply. It is God who has made sexual interaction delightful.

Granted this evangelical orientation, I find it hard to justify the often obsessive concern with sexual morality that has developed in modern Christian history. Augustine's "love and do what you will" is a helpful reminder of a proper balance and common sense. Certainly, people need instruction and encouragement if they are to use their sexuality well, as they need instruction and encouragement if they are to use their material wealth well. Still, a certain amount of trial and error usually is necessary before they find their stride and get onto the road to wisdom. We ought to trust that ordinary Christians can find stirrings of the Holy Spirit to guide them, and so we ought to spend more time helping them learn how to pray (deal with the Holy Spirit well) than drilling them in ethical do's and don'ts.

Concerning independence of mind, autonomy

to employ their time and talent as they find best, laypeople ought also to make the Holy Spirit their first counselor. They have been "anointed" with the Spirit in all the sacraments. They should be experiencing the action of the Spirit as repair and nourishment through participating regularly in penance and the eucharist. In all their spiritual effort, the Spirit of Christ works as their paraclete—the helper whom the resurrected Jesus promised. The private prayer life of any Christian, lay or religious, depends on this promise. Always we have available in our depths the mysterious presence of the Spirit. Certainly, we must let the Spirit teach us, sometimes painfully, what is God's will. But at both sunrise and eventide—whenever and wherever we "come to ourselves"—the Spirit is pouring forth God's love in our hearts with sighs too deep for words. For the Spirit is the deepest stratum of the currents in our spirits. All patterns of thought or feeling or volition rest on her divine movements. We belong to her, to God. God never lets us go. The more deliberately we belong, and the more sensitively we respond to God's initiatives, the freer we become.

Jesus, who became as free as we can imagine, was led by the Spirit to want only the will of his Father. Not his own will, but what the Father wanted, determined his life. We learn what God (Father, Son, and Spirit) wants by examining what happens to us and our world—asking the Spirit to help us sift out our experience. Success or failure, pleasure or pain—either can come from God; either can serve God. God asks all of us for a blank check. Simply by being human, we all have laid on us the full charge of what a saintly life requires. This is only to love God with our whole minds, hearts, souls, and strengths, and to love our neighbors as ourselves. Alternatively, holiness only requires trying to do the will of God and accepting what providence dispenses. Each of us has a unique path to walk, a peculiar cross to carry. It profits little to compare them. We do best to give God full trust. If we ask God for bread, we will not receive a stone. If we accept gratefully the vocation God offers, our time can only make us a success.

RELIGIOUS AND PRIESTS

In Christian history there developed a distinction within religious communities that characterized some members (men not ordained, women not taking the most solemn vows) as "lay" brothers or sisters. I take this phenomenon as another indication that the Christian community has not been able to make hard and fast disjunctions among its ranks of members. Thus, priests have been secular (diocesan) or religious, while religious have been lay or clerical or solemnly professed. Such a conceptual messiness is not uncharacteristic of canon law, but here it is not mere dimness of wit. The fact is that the New Testament and, arguably, deepest Christian instinct, worries little about distinguishing disciples into different ranks, kinds, or types. What Christians hold in common is far more important than the forms or rules of life they hold separately.

Here, I am interested in how religious life sheds light on common Christian faith. For such an interest, the potential in the vows for helping one meet God starkly stands out. If poverty is actual, and obedience is genuine, and chastity means an inner solitude neither neurotic nor cold, then one has personal conditions favoring mystagogy and mysticism. Mystagogy is the actuation of our awareness of the mysteriousness of God: the too-fullness, the simplicity, the limitlessness that makes God always greater than what we can grasp. Mysticism is the direct, relatively unmediated experience of God that comes when and as God wishes and that strikes the experient as indubitable. In both mystagogy and mysticism, the world falls away for the moment and God predominates with an unusual clarity.

God is in the world, its creator and redeemer. Christ is in the world, the Logos become flesh. Christian mysticism does not deny these propositions, but it does entail experiencing that the world is not God and God is not the world. It can respond knowingly to the answer that the entirety of creation gave to Augustine: "We are not He." It is a Christian equivalent to the Hindu "*neti, neti*" ("not this, not that"). It rings in the "*nada*" of John of the Cross. No thing is God. No place gives the human spirit adequate rest. The exhilaration in experiencing this comes as a force of liberation. The terror in experiencing it comes as scripture found: It is a terrible thing to fall into the hands of the living God. Religious life can set people up to behold this mystical foundation of all reality and walk out to the brink. Whatever active ministries a particular religious rule may entail, its mystical (or, more tamely, contemplative) core is its source of distinction.

Of course, one does not have to take religious vows or live in a religious community to be drawn by God into mystical matters. Indeed, vows and communal life can become impediments, if people do not make them transparent. In the final analysis, discretion and maturity cut across vocational boundaries, as do the other gifts of God's Spirit. People blessed with contemplative gifts tend to recognize one another, despite differences in upbringing and accoutrement. One can have the mind and heart of a monk while working on Wall Street. One can suffer the dark night of the soul in a mountain hut or facing a mountain of dirty diapers.

In my ideal church, religious life offers Christians a mystical option generation after generation. I find my heart going glad when I contemplate the church's treasuring the desire of a signal few to leave the world and trek through the desert. God is a desert, as well as a tropical forest. God is as invisible as the wind, as simple as a primary number. Yet we can love God like nothing else. We can long for God as for nothing earthly. And this longing can continue for a lifetime, often burning below ground. Anyone habitually disquieted, unsatisfied, aware in the dead of night or at the fine point of her soul that dying is necessary recognizes this burning. It has a gravity, an inertia, carrying us away from the world, giving us a taste of something other. The otherness of God is not a contradiction of the nearness or the enfleshment. Yet it is essential to God's being God. God can contain what for us are antinomies, contradictions, incompatibles. God can take flesh without ceasing to be divine. The Word can "empty" himself without losing a drop. And God can love us all, the teeming billions, not as an indiscriminate mass but one by one, as though moved by our every fingerprint and freckle.

My point is not to romanticize religious life nor hold individual religious to impossible standards. My interest is in having the church as a whole find in religious life something precious—always important for an orthodox faith, worship, and practice.

(Finding this, the church as a whole might see the fittingness, indeed the moral imperative, of supporting financially, in simple circumstances, any religious who work honestly at vowed, contemplative life. I have in mind the current scandal that many aged religious are down and out financially.) An orthodox faith depends on our confessing that there is only one God and that we never understand him, or her, or it. Whatever we say about God, no matter how orthodox, God is always more unlike than like our saying. If we claim to have understood God, we have erred badly. In the medieval fight between Abelard and Bernard, Bernard's mystical gifts compensated for his dialectical deficiencies. He knew that we can never parse God out with syllogisms. Abelard did not know this as well.

Our proper worship also depends on our having sufficient experience of the otherness of God, the godness of God, to make praise our pride. *Te Deum laudamus*—"You, God, we praise." All Christians should throw their mite into the debate about which architecture, music, rituals, and the like are the best means to the end of praising God today. We should all analyze why Chartres does and does not continue to serve our souls well. But we should also ensure that we have strong input from people who find God far from the madding crowd, at the edge of the ocean cliffs, or in the depths of the silent forests.

Consulting them is a good protection against aestheticism. A Cistercian elegance is both rich and simple. A Franciscan poverty mediates a humility that makes us kind. Benedictine work is little different from Benedictine chant. Jesuit sophistication advanced the cause of Alphonsus Rodriguez, a janitor.

These are not perceptions, sensitivities of soul, that you can find in the world. There are no shelves for them at Wal-Mart. They do not hang out with glut, either material or emotional. Always they turn us back to the beginning; keep us aware of the end. The mystical life becomes funny, mirth in the blood. Gold, frankincense, mirth. Religious life should be a pun. To be rebound to God is to suggest the joke that we could ever be unbound. Religion is a conscious umbilical. Religious life is lovely in the measure that it loves for us all what makes God *God.*

Priests may be religious or not, as we have seen. Except in some Protestant churches, they must be males. Historically, priests began as adjutants of bishops—lieutenants in the work of serving the community's good order. This work had a natural tie to the weekly eucharistic assembly, so bishops tended to preside there. But ordination—laying on hands for service—was not a rite designed to sacralize the one whom the community was choosing. Early Christianity did not follow the majority of Hellenistic religions in thinking of the ordained as mediators between heaven and earth. As Paul's Letter to the Hebrews makes clear, in the Christian dispensation Christ is the only high priest, and the entire church (Christ, head and members) continues Christ's work, especially through its word and sacrament.

Saying this need not overlook the function of the ordained in preaching the word, administering the sacraments, or directing the community for good order. It simply reminds us that the whole community is the repository or focus of Christ's continuing work. In good ecclesiology, the prime focus is not the small clerical portion of the church. Saying this also reminds us that those in orders are no more sacral than the rest of the baptized, just as religious are no more mystical than laypeople. Each Christian vocation has its own dignity and perils. The happiest situation results when what is common (the life of God) bulks larger than what is particular. Then the vocations can complement one another rather than than compete.

In this context, the historian of Christian ministry, Edward Schillebeeckx, finds much to lament in the sacralization of the Catholic priesthood that arose in the Counter-Reformation. I find it lamentable that the gritty humanity present in the evangelical portraits of Jesus gave way in modern times to an otherworldly, spiritualized profile for the representatives of Jesus. Mandatory celibacy has been only one aspect of this sacralization. Bernard Cooke's full historical study of Christian symbols, *The Distancing of God,* suggests the broader cultural evolution. The result has been an effective clericalization of "the church," shown, for example, in the term's coming to refer in Catholic circles less to the full body of believers than to the ordained members running it. Indeed, the popular term for the upper ranks of the ordained, "the hierarchy," suggests that ordinary laypeople have become lowlanders—the base of a great pyramid. However, a church so dominated by people in orders that only they figure much in its operative self-understanding is an engine firing on only a few of its cylinders.

This relates to the criteria for ordination. In the Roman Catholic church, where the criteria have come to include being male and celibate, the pool of available talent is now small from the outset. Perhaps 90 percent of the membership is not eligible for orders, need not even be considered when the community gathers to discern who ought to lead it. This guarantees that Roman Catholic leadership will not be the best and the brightest. Although the link between the phrase "the best and the brightest" and the American disaster in Vietnam can raise bells of alarm, in itself this expression can serve as a neat summary of what any sane community ought to seek when it selects its leaders. It ought to want those most intelligent, discreet, and gifted by God—primed for holiness. To make any other criteria primary is to subvert good sense and so make it likely that leadership of one's community will be mediocre.

It is true that the Christian church is open to all comers and can never be elitist in a pejorative sense. It should not be true that the church nourishes despisers of human culture, any more than it should be true that secular societies nourish what Schleiermacher called "cultural despisers of religion." *"Excellence"* is not a dirty word, although *"arrogance"* is. Christians should find in their community a humble commitment to excellence—one more impressive, more edifying, than what they find in the world. They should find an appreciation of talent and faith that turns people into viable candidates for leadership regardless of their sex, age, marital status, race, ethnic background, sexual orientation, or other secondary characteristic. What is the apparent faith of this person—the depth and clarity of his or her calling from God? What is the intelligence, maturity, experience, social skills, moral character? These are the obvious questions to ask, the straightforward criteria to employ. The burden of proof falls on those who would employ any others.

Granted all this, it is pleasant to contemplate how the ordained, the members of the Christian priesthood, would ideally conceive of their work. Since "evangelization" has been much on the mind of Pope John Paul II recently and bears on such work, let me suggest a distinction that may clarify the balance at work in the best priestly spiritualities. On the one hand, the ordained ought to feel a burning need to preach the gospel, and so they ought to think of their ministerial services dynamically. Christians have good news to offer, and any people with eyes to see, ears to hear, can appreciate its relevance.

However, the work of getting the gospel to take hold so as to transform people's souls and cultures belongs to God more than ourselves. To the degree that we acknowledge our dependence on the Spirit of God, our efforts at evangelization will become less driven, more graceful, and so, effective. Worry does no good. Straining bends things out of shape. Our job is less to bring God to a given situation than to second the work of God already in place. People cannot be human without God. Whatever is true, noble, good, upbuilding in their culture comes from God and solicits our support. We should worry less about getting people to think in overtly Christian categories than about getting them to be honest and loving. If we really believe that Jesus the Christ is the fullest revelation of humanity as well as of divinity, we shall deal with all human cultures respectfully.

The priests who do best are those who encourage all their people to grow more human through faith. They want honesty from their people, not canned responses. They respect moral struggle more than fabricated compliance with customary mores. Wise leaders in the church know that helping people mature in prayer is a two-edged sword. The more fully people come to rely on the Holy Spirit, the less wooden their obedience can be. The gamble of any experienced teacher or parent is that the process of education, the dynamic of the examined life, serves the ends of God. Let our people follow their consciences responsibly and they will get to the places God desires.

The last hallmark I would stress for the ordained is joy. Those who lead the Christian community ought to be signal for their deep contentment. Certainly, life is hard for many people—only fools would deny it. But joy is compatible with suffering. Though physical pain can make joy hard to feel, spiritual pain coexists regularly with joy. The average performance of human beings, myself included, makes most examinations of conscience bittersweet. In a healthy Christian faith, however, our works do not command the center. Rather, we have the relief of looking outward, to the beauty of God. The beauty of God is our birthright, part of our human code. In the worst of our moods, it can slip in, making us forget ourselves. Looking toward God, we remember that all can never be lost. In God nothing is lost, except our sins. Priests who serve us forgiveness and eucharistic nourishment do the best of good works. They deserve well of us and God all their days.

FAMILIAL GOVERNANCE: BISHOP AND POPE

In an ideal church, the community of Christ is a family affair, an association bred in the bone, carried in the blood. We begin where our parents stand. Theirs are the hands that lift us over for baptism, when we begin lucky. Theirs are the fingers we have to ungnarl if our spirits start out in knots. We ought to find in the community of Christ something intimate like familial knowledge, something deep like our marrow. Faith ought to be thicker than water—body and blood of Christ our Lord. Whatever cordons we require for order ought to be only ways to keep the traffic flowing. The style of most church business should be informal, relaxed, making us feel at home. A good bishop gives informality and warmth an imprimatur. It is a trace of Christ he has made his own. He is happiest when with his people. They are happiest when he is around. This good feeling cuts problems (money, discipline) down to size. The poor are always with us. A few family members will always act out. If they are *our* poor, *our* dented relatives, there is a good chance we shall get them solid help.

A bishop is more than the first among equals in a local community, of course. He or she is also a link to the apostolic generation and a guardian of the entire ecumenical community. Bishops constitute a college. Their style of interacting ought to be collegial, collaborative. Competition among bishops has no more place than competition between laypeople and religious. It makes sense for bishops to have enclaves where they can unbutton their troubles to their peers. But the need for this should be minimal, because their usual style of governance should be informal, unstarched. Certainly, the liturgical traditions that have developed represent an aesthetic and theological treasury worth safeguarding. Even the costumes have instructive historical value. But originally most of the costumes were not outlandish and so did not distance the officiants from the ordinary faithful. Any otherness focused on the mysteries being celebrated and came from their being divine. Even there, however, people found a comforting sameness, for these were always the mysteries of Christ our God—of divinity come in our own flesh. So any transfer of sacral distance to the presiding bishop risked losing much in translation. It is God who is other because holy. A fellow Christian who is holy becomes other only by being more human, and so more attractive, than the rest of us.

The forms of address, the habits of speech we

use when dealing with our bishops are a tip-off to how we think about them. Simple *"bishop"* is a good word, when a first name would be too informal. Similar rules hold for dress. What is a mode of apparel that shows who the leader is (when that information is relevant) without making him marginal, let alone peculiar? On the whole, a plain business suit, often recognizably clerical, would seem the best garb. Rings, pectoral crosses, and flashes of color at the collar are minor touches best left to individual taste. Episcopal robes should be left for the few occasions properly formal, much like academic ones. Now and then a procession in pomp and circumstance provides theater. It loses drama if it becomes customary.

For liturgical occasions, form should follow function. Any eucharistic assembly ought first to be a messianic banquet, a plain but happy memorial meal. The music, incense, bells, and candlelight ought to pay their way as helps to a prayerful celebration of this compact symbol of faith. Jesus our pasch gives himself for us once again. The main motif is joyful. The minor chords are sad. The more effective the eucharistic liturgy, the better the reprise of faith with which people leave. In this regard, a Protestant or Zen spareness now delights my Catholic soul. At the center Christ would hold the most prominent sway, bodied forth in the grace of the bishop.

Last, when I think of the bishop as a teacher, his accent is pastoral. It is well for bishops to be good technical theologians and lamentable that few are. It is more important that bishops have the charism to discern what the basic creed means for their people here and now. A bishop who can read the signs of the times can be a very effective leader. One of the best means to this end is listening carefully. A fine example is Archbishop Weakland's going round to the women of Milwaukee. Tired of muffled translations, he wanted to hear their troubles at first hand. There is a time to speak, even a time to command, but it comes after careful listening. Liberation theology reminds us that the people most expert about a problem are the ones suffering from it. If you want to know about welfare, pay more heed to people stuck in the system than to economists and statisticians. If you are serious about reforming health care, listen to the patients and medical personnel living on the front lines. It is not hard to meet representative experts in a given diocese. Their numbers are quite finite. The main requisite is understanding one's mission so as to make listening to the experts central. The wise do not speak without having listened.

A bishop is a leader at the service of all God's people in the area—which is to say, of all the people there. It is not peripheral for a bishop to deal with the city hospitals or jails, the public schools or councils of art. Whatever makes an impact on the common weal, the culture at large, is grist for a bishop's mill. This does not mean he should not concentrate on precisely Christian pastoral theology. It just means that ideally a bishop writes his column, conducts his radio or TV show, plans her board meetings, schedules her lectures and public appearances, with the universal good in mind. A provocative principle of late scholastic thought, influential in the missionary strategy of the first Jesuits, was that a good is divine in the measure that it is universal. In the sixteenth century, this made an argument for concentrating on higher education (the *college*). By the same principle, a bishop does best when making a steady, honest impact on the entire life of his diocese, secular as well as religious.

Inevitably, bishops have to solicit financial support for the good works of the church in their charge, and this brings them into parlous contacts with the wealthy. In such contacts they ought to strive for a keen awareness, one helping them grow wise as serpents and innocent as doves. A good point on which to focus their attention is *influence*. What influence are they offering to handsome donors, and what influence are such donors seeking? Much in this area is subtle, tacit, slow to develop, but little is unimportant. Ideally, a bishop is at home with the wealthy inasmuch as they display a cultured Christian sensibility, but ill at ease inasmuch as they overvalue mammon. Relatedly, the politics of the wealthy can be tricky, a wrongful conservatism expressing a desire to protect a privileged status quo, sometimes at the expense of social justice. Indeed, such a political conservatism can look for support from a conservative theology. Almost always, a proper pastoral theology is neither conservative nor liberal. A proper pastoral theology is usually gently radical: wholehearted love of God (to the detriment of mammon) and love of neighbor as self (to the detriment of antagonisms between social classes). The bishop who ventures forth with courage, trusting in the Holy Spirit, and who returns to the chapel for a quiet half hour can get a fine education. Over the years, such seasoning can bring out in his leadership a fine grain.

The bishop of Rome gained preeminence in the early church for two reasons. The first was the status of Rome as the leading city of the Empire that for the early Christians defined the range of the cultured world. The second was the reputation of Rome for doctrinal purity. Thus, Pope Leo I was the umpire in some crucial Christological controversies, while the memory of the deaths of Peter and Paul in the capital made the Roman church arguably the most apostolic. Recently the ecumenical movement has spotlighted the potential of the Petrine ministry to symbolize the unity of the worldwide Christian community.

We have reflected on the mark or note of unity that has long characterized ideal reflections on the church. Although one can develop several ways of expressing this unity, both historical and doctrinal, the Petrine ministry merits serious consideration. Assuming that unity is a serious desire among all Christians, even though our history makes this assumption dubious, one can say that the Petrine ministry ought to be attractive to all Christians. One has only to hear the words of the Johannine Jesus (John 17) with a docile ear to ground this inference. If the desire of the Johannine Jesus that his followers be one has any moral authority, then the services of the Petrine ministry become desirable.

In noting the worldwide responsibilities of bishops, we spoke of the collegial character of the episcopate. The Petrine ministry is not an independent service. It ought to take place in concert with the ministries of the pope's fellow bishops. The bishop of Rome ought to be the first among a college of equals. Many commentators on the Second Vatican Council spoke of it as completing a theological rationale left incomplete by Vatican I. In Vatican I the emphasis had fallen on the prerogatives of the bishop of Rome. In Vatican II, the complementary teachings filled out the collegiate character of the episcopal office as a whole.

And even though both conciliar discussions ran the risk of making the church appear to be a clerical operation, such that the function of the 90 percent of the body who are lay would be of secondary significance, taken together, they could have the positive benefit of clarifying how the pope in concert with the bishops might best function minsterially for the well-being of the entire body of Christ.

In the last years of the twentieth century, the actual functioning of the Petrine ministry, through its various Vatican offices, has not been altogether fortunate. Ordinary Christians who look to Rome for warmth and encouragement have often found the official visage chilling. Every office in the church ought always to be in humble dialogue with others, consulting the faithful in matters of doctrine and morals, making sure that local ordinaries have the main say in the interpretation of faith in their jurisdictional area. The principle of subsidiarity, much honored in Catholic texts on church governance but sputtering in the daily politics of the Vatican in the 1990s, says that Christians ought to settle matters at the most local level possible, because that is where the requisite expertise is easiest to acquire. A rightful adaptation of the principle of diversity or multiculturalism says that to appoint only bishops of a conservative cast of mind is to do the body of Christ a great disservice.

Inasmuch as in the 1990's a lockstep mentality seemed to settle over Rome, with bishops appointed by litmus tests that included opposition to both the ordination of women and changes in the rules about priestly celibacy, people of deep faith had to question the de facto orthodoxy of the Vatican leadership. Regularly, it seemed to be willing to default on its primary obligation—to furnish the faithful with eucharistic word and sacrament—so as to uphold quite secondary, man-made legal conventions. This disorder gave objective grounds for doubting the pastoral competence of those holding the highest offices in the Roman Catholic communion. Obviously, such a judgment did little to enhance the prospect of plumping for the bishop of Rome as the point man for ecumenical reunion.

We show our actual faith in the priority of grace, the primacy of the Holy Spirit, by going gently with the consciences of others, by inclining always to dialogue rather than command. Moreover, among our various obligations few are more pressing than the claim on us by God to make our faith an honest expression of Jesus' good news. We have no right to be sour, pessimistic purveyors of judgment and doom. If Christ is risen, the worst of our impasses has to be penultimate. If we genuinely believe that where sin abounded grace has abounded the more, we have to grant all believers full liberty of conscience in which to celebrate this existential hopefulness. The first Peter told those who were harassing him, "We must obey God rather than men." What has changed in twenty centuries to make that statement impertinent for Christians today?

The fact is that in twenty centuries the barque of Peter has collected many barnacles. Things that are quite doubtful have inserted themselves as pretenders to existence by divine right. An ideal church that accepted the New Testament principle that judgment begins with the household of God and that saw the rightfulness of the Reformers' precept that the church has always to be reformed would scrape such barnacles away gladly, with vigor. The vast majority of customs that have grown up in the Christian community are historically conditioned and accidental— things not necessary but dubious. Regarding them, Christians with the courage to claim it have great liberty. A properly functioning Petrine ministry would be first in promoting this liberty. It would think of itself as the champion of all Christians' free consciences, the servant of the primacy of the Holy Spirit in all believers' hearts. And so it would minimize its own claims, titles, rights, importances. Just as in a healthy family the father and mother seldom stand on ceremony or dignity, so in a healthy church the leaders blush to be thought self-important.

In the buzz of the outside world, the rap on the

papacy is that it preaches better than it practices. It has a fine line about social justice, but if you examine how things actually go in the schools and hospitals under its control, you will find less than ideal labor practices. It speaks eloquently about the dignity of women, but if you ask Catholic (or Orthodox) hierarchs what access to the inner sanctums of church power they offer to women, you will have to work hard to keep a straight face. Too many church leaders have colluded with military butchers in Latin America and Serbia to make pronouncements from their mountaintops fully credible. Reports of too many pedophiles and financial irregularities have hit the headlines to allow cardinals their old bluster. If you visit Vatican City, you will take the preferential option for the poor with a grain of salt. (You may also remember Luther's momentous visit.) If you study the history of relations between church and state in Eastern Christianity, you will have to say that for every badge of heroism there has been a shameful patch of acquiescence.

None of this means that the Petrine ministry does not carry great potential for serving the future unification of the churches. All of it simply argues that church leaders in all three major branches have tended to get above themselves and forget who is Lord. The community of Christ needs people willing to spend themselves for its well-being. Often that is a thankless job, bringing them abuse they do not deserve. They deserve neither abuse nor adulation. There should be no hermeneutic of suspicion, savaging all their pronouncements out of an anticlerical hatred, but also no cult of personality, verging on idolatry. Our leaders are simply human beings. The sacredness of the God whom they serve does not make them sacral dolls. We should pray for them and be grateful for their self-spending. We should not take any guff from them, but we should try to appreciate how hard it is for public figures to keep their balance. They need to laugh at themselves, and we need to laugh with them. The more keenly they appreciate the distance between themselves and their Lord, without letting that depress them, the more winning their laughter will be.

The medieval popes, epitomized by the Borgias, show the nadir to which the Petrine ministry can fall. The recent popes, clustered around the Second Vatican Council, offer us much to admire. With false starts and failures of nerve and strange maladroitnesses about public relations, they have nonetheless eased the way for the Roman Catholic communion to work out a quite new self-understanding as de facto a worldwide church. No religious communion has taken this challenge more fully to heart. Islam has no center comparable to the papacy, nor has Hinduism,

Buddhism, or Judaism. Despite the fractures in the Christian community, enough goodwill among Protestants and Orthodox keeps the symbolism of Rome truly ecumenical. With a little flexibility all around and a keener appreciation of the sinfulness of their divisions, Christians in all three major church families could come together significantly, indeed, dramatically. If they really wanted, they could make the twenty-first century the time when the bishop of Rome served as the symbolic center of the entire ecumenical communion, outstanding for his selfless love of the whole. That would be a millennial achievement indeed.

FORM: INSTITUTIONAL AND CHARISMATIC

We have been looking at the different ranks or circles or vocations in the Christian community. Implicit throughout has been a dialectical relationship between aspects that we can call institutional and aspects that we can call charismatic. Such a terminology is not completely adequate or felicitous, but it can serve us well enough to round out our theological reflection. The Christian church has virtually inevitably developed a far-flung, complicated, institutional or organizational apparatus. There are offices, secretariats, bureaus, and the like at the headquarters and through the ranks of all the major church families. There are chanceries and committees and officials in all the patriarchates, dioceses, synods, and other smaller jurisdictions. Each church has its canon laws, manuals of discipline, custom books, rules and regulations—enough to give Qoheleth a new headache. We have masters of ceremonies, and administrators of national conferences, and chapters for religious, and organizations for lay Christians. This is what I mean by the institutional side of church life. Clearly, it involves the community in management, financial planning, public relations, and—high, low, and middle—politics. This is inevitable, though probably not so inevitable, let alone so desirable, as some busy Christians have come to assume. Indeed, if there is a constant feature in the movements for reform that have arisen regularly in church history, it is a cry from the heart for simplification: a return to the bare beginnings.

I think that the healthiest state of affairs, the ideal posture, is for the institutional side of things to love and honor the charismatic side, thinking of itself as so much effort to make straight the prophets' path. Correlatively, the charismatic side of things is most winning when it shows itself appreciative of all that is necessary to keep going the community that the Spirit would enliven: the money, the buildings, the soap and wax and elbow grease. Any monk not digging his own vegetables, not pounding together his own hut, not boiling his own bath water has to pray for his benefactors, not as a pious, supererogatory act, but out of plain obligatory gratitude. He could not do what he is doing, could not be what he is being, without the alms, and so, the work of others. On the other hand, a church without monks, nuns, hospitals, schools, chaplaincies, and the rest would be an emaciated body of Christ. Most of the apparatus, the tradition, that we have developed is quite defensible. It needs pruning or repair more than razing. Alfred North Whitehead said that we should seek simplicity and distrust it. He was referring to cosmological theory, but his saying applies just as well to church reform. If not this apparatus, this system of chanceries, this canon law, then some other—because we simply are not able to make do with inspiration, pneumatic concord, alone.

The struggle for balance gains its ecclesiological justification from the incarnation. God has not made us angels but enfleshed, historical, social beings. God has not made the supreme revelation of the divine love a mist around the moon but the smooth skin and bright eyes of the baby Jesus, the ironic laugh of Jesus the wandering preacher and healer, the broken body of the crucified Jesus, the wonderful presence of the resurrected Jesus known at the breaking of the bread. *If* this choice by God, *then* sex and food and economics and politics and pain and dance. We have to get together—loins to loins, buyers to sellers, students to teachers, dead to buriers. Under analysis, the institutional side of Christian communal life is very ordinary, fully human. It happens in Sicilian families, in Madagascar, and at the UN. Every burg and borough has its traffic laws, its stamps and nails and taxes. How could the church be an exception? Where could Christians get another skin?

What should be clearer in the church than in most other places, though, is the, at most, penultimate character of all this stuff. The liturgy needs some rubrics, but it is stupid to say that these given ones bind under mortal sin. Good order requires that all bow at the same time, but for monsignor (or director of liturgy) to start snapping fingers pushes things over the top. Moreover, there are matters straddling the boundary between the institutional and the charismatic that ought to emerge differently in church situations than they might in purely secular ones. For example, when two people decide that their marriage is dead, no longer helping either of them more than it hurts, then in the church the legal/institutional ought to cede to the personal/charismatic. Any "defender of the bond" becomes obnoxious, once all have recalled that marriage is a serious business for faith. Equally obnoxious is any supervening grantor of nullities, come to announce that the marriage never was. The marriage was, and then it died or fell apart or became dysfunctional. The honest thing would be to honor its actual history, setting that in the context of Christian penance and hope.

Divorce does not defeat God any more than does any other undesirable happening or experience. Pedophilia does not defeat God. There can be life after being named a bishop. Hurt or funny or cynical, we can all still drag our carcasses before God. This fundamental conviction of our faith means that all the procedures of our courts and lawyers and therapists are less than the final word. The final word is hidden in God with Christ Jesus our Lord. The last and ultimately only important judgments are all claims on God's mercy. That is why the institutional side of things ought always to be humble and self-effacing. Respect for institutional things, yes. Worship of institutional things, no. A lot of ecclesiastical wisdom lies in knowing the difference.

In moving toward this wisdom, we are blessed to have the evangelists' portraits of Jesus' struggles. On the one hand, he did not want to denigrate the Torah. It was precious in his sight, in his soul, and he wanted to honor it more than criticize it. On the other hand, he was put off by many of the current interpretations of the Torah, as his battles with some of the Pharisees suggest. One influential interpretation of the killing of Jesus ties it to the hatred that his challenge to the Law, and so to the religious establishment, aroused. People in power, having come to think well of themselves, could not abide a serious challenge to their self-image. It made them furious to find crowds going after Jesus because they delighted in both his power to heal and the free-spiritedness of his preaching. He was a breath of fresh air. In his presence people felt wonderfully liberated. Jealous of this impact and fearing the demise of their own influence, the enemies of Jesus declared his followers a dirty rabble and him a danger to public order. The terrible judgment that it was better for one man to die than for the people as a whole to perish—power politics at its most cynical—may not actually have been uttered. But the New Testament leaves no doubt that the early Christians assimilated Jesus to the Suffering Servant of Second Isaiah—the innocent victim of human malice whose death turned out to be redemptive.

How? In part by revealing the depths to which human depravity had fallen, the mindlessness to which hatred of human goodness had traveled. It is perilous to venture parallels with later historical phenomena such as the Nazi holocaust of millions of Jews, but it is salutary to recognize that one of the factors allowing that twentieth-century enormity was the Christian replication of the mentality of the enemies of Jesus, through centuries of hating Jews mindlessly. People who confuse laws or established cultural outlooks or statuses quo concerning power with the will of God are always making themselves liable to mindless hatreds. When we consider the institutional side of communal Christian life we should not let ourselves forget the demons shrieking in our history, the devil who quotes scripture in our own breasts.

Charismata are gifts of the Holy Spirit. The apostle Paul, analyzing church life a generation after Jesus, takes it for granted that such gifts abound. Indeed, the problem is to keep them in good order, lest they tumble over one another. There is a hierarchy in such gifts. Some are more important than others. Teaching and prophecy are more important than speaking in tongues. The gifts that build the community up are more important than the gifts that only benefit individuals. Indeed, according to Paul, the greatest of the charismata is charity.

We have come in sight of this conclusion repeatedly in the saying, "In necessary things unity; in doubtful things, liberty; and in all things, charity." We know that charity is the substance of the twofold commandment by which Jesus summarized the Law and Prophets: love of God, with whole mind, heart, soul, and strength, and love of neighbor as self. God is love, according to the Johannine theology. Those who abide in love abide in God and God abides in them. The most crucial sign of Christ's gift of the Spirit is his disciples' abiding in love—their stable affection. People who are loving and honest—warm and clear—are moved, held, purified by the Spirit, almost despite themselves. They may think that they are poor disciples, even no believers at all. The transparency of their goodness, the fineness of their behavior and affection, betrays them. The various charismata—gifts to preach, teach, heal, lead, pray—are so many expressions of the charity of Christ, his love both urgent and peaceful.

Urgent: the Spirit of Christ makes missionaries, evangelizers, workers. Disciples in love with Christ, enamored of his God, are restless to let the world know about the kingdom of God, to transform the institutions of society so that they become compatible with this kingdom. *Peaceful:* the work of spreading the good news belongs to God, depends on God, more than ourselves. We cannot change our height a cubit. We have no power to move people to repentance, to replace their hearts of stone with hearts of flesh. Paul watered, Apollos planted, but God gave the increase. We do what we can, what we think best. The results lie out of our hands, often out of our knowing.

You give a talk or a homily. People come up afterwards, saying this and that. But you leave with no idea of what good you did, what problems you caused. You write an article and send it off to a fate you cannot monitor. Who reads it, to what effect, is a great mystery. It is amazing to learn, now and then, that someone found a lifeline in paragraphs that you now barely remember. There is little in this mysteriousness peculiar to theologians. Doctors do what they can and never know the overall impact. They can know that a shattered arm has healed, or failed to do so, but they can know little about a patient's soul. Equally, parents have to live by faith, giving their counsels, administering their punishments, offering their encouragements largely in the dark. Why does one child thrive and another get into scrape after scrape? What makes Annie happy and Tom so mournful? From the chemistry at work in our blood to the chances that make up our educations, our love lives, our successes and failures at work, we live and move and have our being in a providential mystery. The Spirit of God is not extrinsic—egg wash at the end to give the baked loaf a tan. The Spirit of God—divine providence, charismata, grace—is a crucial part of the whole process. It is the leaven, the vitamin, perhaps even the protein or carbohydrate without which we starve. It is the oxygen, the light, the spiritual medium without which we would have no thought or will or religious emotion. It is easier to say where the Spirit is than to be sure where it is not. It is harder to set boundaries to its operation than to deny that it is always at work.

The church that only pays the Spirit lip service is immature in the extreme. It is a community that does not know what it is about—its foundation or constitution. The Spirit, God-given and received (in virtue of Christ, as Christians see things), comes before, is always more basic, and continues long after any of us has left the scene. It is the Spirit as charity or love that gives the church its unity. According to Rahner, love is not merely found *in* the church but is constitutive of the church. Were we to take this to heart it would ameliorate much of the antagonism between liberal and conservative. Applying Rahner's dictum, each member of our ideal church would freely follow her conscience. She would fear no sanction unless her deeds were clearly sinful. Her ecclesial birthright of scripture and tradition, sacramental and liturgical support, and prayerful discernment would be accompanied by a presumption of graceful orthodoxy, generous freedom. In such a community, she would have learned early to grant others similar liberty. Our daily prayer—as a church—would be for the grace to love one another unconditionally. Crabbed conformity would be a sin against the Holy Spirit.

When God chose to become God for us, the Spirit became a circulation in the depths of our love. What most makes us ourselves is now not our own but God's. We know and love and are in God. Our knowing and loving and being are more divine than created, because God has chosen to take us into the divine life and light and love. How this can happen we cannot say. That it has happened, does happen, the evangelical Jesus has said. His saying this ought to be enough for us. His saying this ought to make the charismatic side of the church primary. The church is always human, and always it is fair, indeed necessary, to consider carefully what the church is doing in history. But the ultimate significance of the church rests in dynamics of God that history does not contain and that we cannot fully calculate. A mundane proof of this is the diversity evident in church history: no school or trend or theology ever emerged wholly and exclusively correct. Do we doubt the Spirit's wisdom in willing such multiplicity?

As we conclude our thought-experiment, let's bring this conviction to bear on our analyses of word and sacrament, the primary forms through which the community of Christ expresses itself. Preaching is a charismatic work, depending on the inspiration of God for its ultimate success. God must give the preacher the light and warmth, the unction, necessary to proclaim a word that is salvific. God must also shape the minds and hearts of the people listening to the sermon if it is to take hold and bring forth good yield. The preaching itself ought to be compatible with these pneumatic realities. The preacher ought to prepare it in a spirit of prayer, letting the scriptural words soak into his or her heart through *lectio divina*. The people ought to receive the sermon at a moment in the liturgy when preliminary prayers and music have brought them to suitable dispositions.

The sermon should not be over-long, lest human words or rhetorical strategies begin to dominate. It can be humorous but it should never be pedestrian—never not be distinct from secular talks, let alone secular entertainments. A sermon properly charismatic is not an academic lecture. Neither is it an undisciplined outpouring, an extempore venting. A sermon properly pneumatic is simple but well prepared, cogent yet poetic. It uses words to defeat words and make plain the primacy of God's silence. It evokes a beauty, a range of reality, beyond the quotidian because it is touched by eternity.

Similar qualities attend sacramental rituals that deserve the high adjective "spirit-filled." A eucharistic rite that does justice to the memory of Jesus at table with the twelve, or breaking bread for the multitude, or prefiguring the messianic banquet, or steeling himself for his trial on the cross makes the gestures and symbolic elements transparent. It invites all the participants to move with the Spirit in memory to the intimate love with which Jesus gave himself, body and blood, for his disciples—both the original twelve and all of us who have come later. The eucharist is not a passion play. The priest is not on stage playing Jesus. (The argument that priests must resemble Jesus physically displays a poverty of sacramental understanding.) The eucharist (and any other sacramental rite, *mutatis mutandis*) is a mystagogy: a re-initiation by the Spirit, a re-turn to the historical enfleshment of the love of God that works our repair and divinization.

The institutions of the Christian community exist principally to prepare, support, and carry out the practical implications of such a mystagogy. The center of church life is the encounters with God that work the forgiveness of our sins and the divinizing of our entire selves. Foremost among these are the public gatherings structured by scriptural word and eucharistic sacrament. Also important are the times of prayer and social action that invite the Spirit of God into our spirits and neighborhoods. All Christians are radically equal in their need for the ministrations of the Spirit and their right to cooperate with them. The differences in our gifts are secondary. They are also necessary, if we are to make the community of Christ as diverse and omnipresent as solid Christian instinct has long thought it should be. So at the end of the day (and our meditation), ideal church life depends for its vitality on our sensitivity to the movements of God in our midst. We best approach the liberty of the children of God when we make the Holy Spirit our rule.

This is not a call for quietism or fatalism. It is a plain acknowledgment of the way that things are: mysterious. Grace allows us to confront the mysteriousness of all existence face-to-face and respond with praise for God's glory. *Te Deum laudamus:* you, God, we praise—only you. Hard as it can be in times of pain or abandonment, we praise you. Easy as your grace can make now and then, we exult at the beauty of your world and infer that your beauty must be many times greater. You are beautiful, God, and all creation rightly gives you praise. We pray that you let us praise you all our days, unto the consummation of your church and your world.

SUGGESTIONS FOR
FURTHER READING

In drawing up this list, I was torn between offering *authors* or *titles*. I decided to do both. First, here are the names of some writers whose works are orthodox and creative, prayerful and playful: William Barry, S.J., Lisa Sowle Cahill, Anne Carr, Andre Dubus, Rosemary Haughton, Elizabeth A. Johnson, Mary Jo Weaver, and Paul Wilkes. Read anything they write and you will always have grist for your own thought-experiments.

Now, let me offer a few (mostly recent) titles to continue our conversation about the shape and feel of an ideal church:

Joseph Cardinal Bernardin's *The Gift of Peace: Personal Reflections* (Loyola Press, 1997)

John Carmody's *Cancer and Faith* (Twenty-Third Publications, 1995); *God Is No Illusion* (Trinity Press International, 1997)

Anne Carr's *Transforming Grace* (Harper and Row, 1988)

Bernard Cooke's *The Future of Eucharist* (Paulist Press, 1997)

Lawrence S. Cunningham and Keith J. Egan's *Christian Spirituality: Themes from the Tradition* (Paulist Press, 1996)

Harvey Egan, S.J.'s *Karl Rahner: The Mystic of Everyday Life* (Crossroad, 1998)

Heinrich Fries and Karl Rahner's *Unity of the Churches: An Actual Possibility* (Paulist Press and Fortress Press, 1985)

Elizabeth A. Johnson's *She Who Is* (Crossroad, 1992); *Friends of God and Prophets* (Continuum, 1998)

Catherine LaCugna's *God for Us* (HarperCollins, 1991); *Freeing Theology* (Harper San Francisco, 1993)

Grace Mojtabai's *Soon* (Zoland Books, Inc., 1998)

Karl Rahner's *I Remember* (Crossroad, 1985)

Andrew Sullivan's *Love Undetectable* (Alfred A. Knopf, 1998)

The Madeleva Lecture in Spirituality

This series, sponsored by the Center for Spirituality, Saint Mary's College, Notre Dame, Indiana, honors annually the woman who as president of the college inaugurated its pioneering graduate program in theology, Sister M. Madeleva, C.S.C.

1985
Monika K. Hellwig
Christian Women in a Troubled World

1986
Sandra M. Schneiders
Women and the Word

1987
Mary Collins
Women at Prayer

1988
Maria Harris
Women and Teaching

1989
Elizabeth Dreyer
Passionate Women: Two Medieval Mystics

1990
Joan Chittister, O.S.B.
Job's Daughters

1991
Dolores R. Leckey
Women and Creativity

1992
Lisa Sowle Cahill
Women and Sexuality

1993
Elizabeth A. Johnson
Women, Earth, and Creator Spirit

1994
Gail Porter Mandell
Madeleva: One Woman's Life

1995
Diana L. Hayes
Hagar's Daughters

1996
Jeanette Rodriguez
Stories We Live
Cuentos Que Vivimos

1997
Mary C. Boys
Jewish-Christian Dialogue

1998
Kathleen Norris
The Quotidian Mysteries